"I recommend this book[let] a [...] resource for anyone wh[o ...] PTSD." - **Anne Cawtho[rn, Psychotherapist]** MSc MBE

"Whether it is you who have suffered trauma in life, or whether you are supporting someone personally, or as part of your work, this book will prove to be invaluable. Written with the utmost respect and understanding for its subject matter, this book offers great insight and gives practical help and advice for dealing with the wide and varied issues associated with trauma. I highly recommend it." - **Tracey Odessa Kane**, Author & Poet

"The simplicity of this booklet reflects the character of its writer in covering a very complex subject. Simple, yet powerful." - **Anthea Fenton**, Author & Creator of Life After Stress, Anxiety & Depression, www.energyorchard.net

From trauma to freedom: How to recover from frightening experiences.

An easy to read booklet that answers those questions you were scared to ask.

Josephine Cropper MSc UKCP

ISBN-13: 978-1519290663

From trauma to freedom: How to recover from frightening experiences

First Printing December 2015

Designed by Josephine Cropper

1 3 5 7 9 10 8 6 4

Acknowledgements

I would like to thank my husband Pete (www.petercropper.co.uk), supportive as always, Quentin Pain (QuentinPain.com) for his amazing knowledge and patience, Cathy and Jane for many hours of discussion, and the many others who have made this book possible.

Contents

HOW TO USE THIS BOOK   6

INTRODUCTION   7

1. TRAUMA   9

2. HOPE   17

3. TRUST   21

4. BODY   24

5. BOUNDARIES   29

6. TRIGGER, FLASHBACK   35

7. DISSOCIATION   39

8. MEMORY   42

9. SHAME   45

10. ANGER   49

11. SELF-ESTEEM   55

12. SPIRITUALITY   61

HOW TO USE THIS BOOK

This book is deliberately short, simple and written in plain, simple English. I have read many books and find it very helpful to make a note of any pages to which I may want to return at a later stage.

I have left blank pages at the end of the book to give you the opportunity to write down anything that resonates with you. Every time you read the book you may find you have different light bulb moments.

If you would like to contact me, you can email me on:-

Email: josephine@jmcpsychotherapy.com

INTRODUCTION

What is trauma?

Trauma is anything that overwhelms and makes you feel out of control and unable to cope. It is not something you can think your way out of because your body "hijacks" you.

Post-Traumatic Stress Disorder develops after a terrifying ordeal involving either physical harm or the threat of physical harm. The person who develops PTSD may have been the one who was harmed, or the harm may have happened to a loved one. Perhaps trauma suffered by a stranger has been witnessed; this could also result in PTSD.

PTSD was first brought to public attention in relation to the suffering of war veterans, but it can result from a variety of traumatic incidents. Mugging, rape, torture, being kidnapped or held captive, child abuse, car accidents, train wrecks, plane crashes, bombings, or natural disasters such as floods or earthquakes can all trigger PTSD.

Common questions/statements following traumatic events are:-

Who can I trust?

Where do I go for help?

Can people see what's going on inside me? I hear people say that they feel flawed, contaminated in some way, stained on the inside.

I think I'm going mad. Can someone please, please help?

I just wish I could have one day without emotional or physical pain. Will I ever feel better?

I'm often asked these questions. Who am I, and why am I writing this booklet?

I have been a psychotherapist for over seventeen years and am passionate in my belief that everyone should receive the right help at the right time.

1. TRAUMA

Support for people affected by trauma is an area which has been overlooked for far too long, and this booklet aims to address this.

This booklet is intended to provide you with hope and to let you know that the effects of trauma need not be a life sentence. There ARE things you can do, ways in which you can heal, and the challenges can be overcome. My wish in writing this is to help those who search, are stuck, and simply have nowhere to go emotionally.

I have seen the suffering of many trauma patients, and through knowledge of specialist skills and experience as well as compassion, I can provide a therapeutic intervention that is focused: one-to-one sessions to help you heal after trauma and to help you reclaim and restore a normal life.

I am asked numerous questions again and again by the people I see who have suffered different types of trauma, which includes sexual abuse.

They live with terror, not week by week or day by day, but hour by hour and minute by long minute.

People have their own ways of coping. Some people can distract themselves while they are at work, and they use a very fragile defence to give the appearance that they are partaking normally in the world.

For others, it's not so simple. As one client said, "Normality, Josephine: I don't even know what that means," and she just looked at me blankly, a dead expression evident in her eyes.

For some people, functioning is as good as it gets, while for others the only option is to not partake at all. They remain within their four walls, cocooned, pretending to live and keeping safe, but this comes at the cost of never knowing joy, fun, laughter, relationships, or feeling freedom.

<u>Why is it an issue?</u>

People are not receiving the help they need. They don't know where to go; they may go to their GP with an assortment of ailments, and they may have a vague diagnosis, because they are "not sure what else it is." They may be on medication to deal with symptoms and this may help them survive the day. However, the situation never improves because the underlying issue is not addressed. Ironically, the more of this sort of vague help they receive, the more convinced they become that there really IS something wrong. At the same time they desperately try to hide their whole experience, which would be difficult to discuss in an ordinary everyday conversation.

Here are some of the questions I'm asked by people just like you:-

<u>Why do I never seem to have any energy?</u>

Too much energy is used by the trauma survivor just trying to keep himself or herself together while dealing with the trauma issues. Everyday life becomes a struggle. It feels as if there is a constant ongoing state of conflict between fight (where the survivor is prevented from escaping from the trauma and its effects because he or she feels the need to fight it) and flight (where the survivor tries to escape). The fight / flight mechanism is a primitive, instinctive response that prepares the body to fight or flee from perceived or real threat to our survival.

Going over the details of the trauma at the beginning of therapy can be destabilising, so it is first necessary to help clients feel safe emotionally and in their body. Often there is no need to address individual traumatic incidents until much later in the therapy – and even then, the incidents must be addressed gradually.

What are the symptoms of PTSD/trauma?

There are many symptoms which may include some or all of the following:

- Angry outbursts

- Sleep issues – too much/too little/nightmares

- Loss of a sense of the future

- Decreased concentration

- Feeling numb

- Hypervigilance

- Depression/irritability

- Avoidance of places/things that remind you of the event

- Chronic pain/headaches

- Feeling unreal or out of the body

- Self-destructive behaviour

- Having intrusive thoughts/inability to think

- Shame/worthlessness/mistrust

- Feeling like the scary event is happening again (flashbacks)

The trauma symptoms affect the type of person the survivor becomes; for example, anger is not just a symptom – it leads to the survivor's becoming an angry person in his or her own eyes.

There is part of the brain that helps us distinguish past from present; however, in trauma the brain works differently. This has been proved by various brain scans.

The trauma might have consisted of an isolated incident – an accident, perhaps, or an isolated incidence of bullying rather than ongoing abuse. I sometimes hear people say, "It was only just…" and they minimise the event and their feelings.

In trauma, time is <u>not</u> a healer, and it is necessary to deal with it now. Trauma responses are driven by the nervous system rather than the memory.

<u>What are the steps to recovery?</u>

There is a clear plan involving logical steps to enable recovery from trauma beginning with education of the impact of trauma on the brain.

The establishment of safety and stabilisation are important; this includes bodily safety, a safe environment and emotional stability. This allows a life in the "here and now" so that the client remembers the trauma rather than reliving it.

There is a set of simple physical exercises called Trauma Relief Exercises to help the body let go of deep chronic patterns. They activate the body's natural mechanism of releasing trauma, thus reducing the time needed for talking therapy.

The survivor is then helped to overcome the fear of traumatic memories so that the memories can be integrated and the survivor can come to terms with the traumatic past. There is no need to go through the full details of the trauma again.

This results in healing and a healthy present, and the trauma is consigned to the past.

Why does it need fixing?

Anyone who has undergone trauma has already suffered enough. The suffering needs to stop. Life needs to begin again, but this process may initially be very slow.

For example, if the trauma arose from sexual abuse, it may have lasted only a few seconds. It may have been a moment where you were watched, or asked to talk about your sex life against your will, or touched where you didn't want to be touched. ALL of this is abuse.

When someone has been violated the world changes for ever, but it is not necessary to confront the abuser or go over all the details. For some survivors that would be helpful and for others not; some don't have a clear memory, but just "know" their body knows. Our bodies have memories, and can give very clear signs to us, and thankfully we are starting to return to an era that is clearer that mind and body are together. They work in harmony, and if there is disharmony such as illness there is a reason for it.

Ant came to see me after spending a long time trying to sort out his various physical issues. These ranged from very bad mouth ulcers resulting in his being barely able to speak to suddenly seeming to be allergic to so much. It was almost as though he was allergic to everyday life. He felt he was unable to go out, because people would stop and stare at him. Not only the physical pain, but also the shame this brought him, was excruciating.

He had decided he was a bad person, and that he "looked" a bad person, and he had virtually given up hope. He came to me almost as a last resort.

Mysterious physical symptoms, poor concentration, disorganisation, and being very prone to distraction are all symptoms associated with trauma.

The aim of therapy is to help the survivor eradicate memories which disrupt daily life, and to realise that the past is the past and the present is the present.

Trauma changes the nervous system; therefore, a full recovery means we need to change or reset the nervous system.

Trauma is not something that just happens in the mind; it is also in the body.

2. HOPE

The most important thing I can say to anyone is, "There is HOPE". I have seen a great many people heal from trauma to a point where they can have relationships, get married, and live a normal, happy, healthy life.

It isn't unusual for any trauma, including sexual abuse, to be remembered only in adulthood. However, growing up there is often the gnawing feeling that something is wrong. Joanne said, "I'd always felt like an alien, but I didn't know why." Some trauma survivors only remember fragments, and in other instances the body may remember where the mind does not; this shows itself in mysterious and unexplained illnesses. Self-belief is needed, and all good therapists will believe the survivor. Careful consideration needs to be given to whether it would be beneficial to disclose the abuse as in this situation some families are supportive and some are sadly not, and the latter situation only adds to the pain. All current abuse involving children – where they might be in danger – must legally be disclosed.

How does healing from trauma happen?

It is not just a random process, and there are many steps to take. However, just as in overcoming grief we rarely move through these steps in a fixed order, and flexibility of approach is required.

Firstly we focus on the effects of trauma, and you learn in very simple, straightforward ways the effects of trauma on your body, brain and nervous system, so you can start to feel that you will be able to take charge of your body. If we understand why we do something, change is always easier.

The medical profession is now realising that a lot of stress-related illnesses such as fibromyalgia and M.E. may be related to trauma.

Psychotherapy can help you understand your triggers and ways in which you can enlarge your window of tolerance.

We look at how you are taking care of your body. Are you keeping yourself safe? Good basic self-care is needed, such as a commitment to stopping self-injury, be that physical or through alcohol and drugs.

A safe environment – for example a non-abusive relationship – is needed to overcome the effects of trauma, so that may be the first aim in therapy. Ways to calm and soothe your body are learned, and healthy boundaries are set, so the full range of emotions is experienced without the feeling of being controlled by them.

In dealing with the past it may not be necessary to go over all the details. It is important, however, to deal with the shame and self-loathing, while living in the "here and now" and staying grounded in the present, moving towards a healthy future to help you discover new resources and notice and connect to good things.

In this way trauma becomes something that happened to you in the past, and you are free to smile and simply be you.

Of course, some issues may take a short time to heal, and some may take longer. Recovery is possible, and life becomes better.

As Mary, a 34-year-old nurse, said, "I've got to choose hope. What else is there?"

You will reach a point where you not only know you are safe but you <u>feel</u> safe and there is no fear of the memory.

3. TRUST

We all have to make decisions on a daily basis about who to trust and who not to trust, and who we can place confidence in and why.

Trust is the strong belief in the reliability, truth, ability or strength of someone or something. Trauma can disrupt trust, and this can have a lasting impact on a person's life.

When a traumatic event is experienced, it is as if the whole value system is changed, and there is uncertainty about who can be trusted.

It is necessary to learn to trust self, and be clear when the inner traumatised voice is swinging between trusting everyone and trusting no one.

"I wasn't sure who to speak to and I was really frightened – even though I was in my late 30s. I started making friends with other people who had been abused, but it was just too much for me – too draining. Internet forums can be useful, but also draining.

For a long, long time I kept going around the houses thinking that maybe tomorrow I could talk about it, and yet at the same time desperately wanting to talk and be heard today. It was tormenting me. I really felt as if I'd done all the wrong and I'd done others harm: the guilt makes you feel like you are going to explode before you tell someone, but who can you trust? I had been badly let down so many times in adult life and I was petrified, and yet like a child I so much needed to reach out and be cared for."

Louise continued, "When you first tell someone, you are on such a high because at last you have done it. It's like being let out of a cage after a very long time in captivity. But then the fear kicks in again and you wonder between sessions whether it was OK to tell that person. You need lots of reassurance."

Therapy will help you understand the differences between healthy and unhealthy friendships and help you to learn how to trust and who to trust.

No reputable therapist will push anyone to tell their story, and the latest research shows that only after trust has been established, and current life issues have been looked at, will the trauma itself be focused on. Even then it will be a very gradual process.

The problem occurs when you have a memory of going to the person to whom you would turn for soothing and it turned out to be wrong and unsafe. It's hard to trust when you have been betrayed. If you are five years old and it is your parent who is abusing you, how do you know who is safe to trust? Where do you go?

Trust builds up slowly. You come to know your healthy boundaries, knowing what will trigger you, and having a strategy to deal with these.

It is difficult to trust if you are hypervigilant. What if you do trust and are let down? This can then lead to shame, and you brand yourself a stupid person.

4. BODY

In trauma, the body itself may have been injured or threatened; we become uncomfortable with our body, or live from our head, disconnected from our body. Becoming positive about our body and learning to listen to it and take care of it are important steps in healing.

People often say, "I hate my body, it disgusts me. I push myself really hard, I need to keep going, and sometimes my body just won't work and it lets me down. I'm always cold."

Phil would regularly attend the session with a new tattoo or piercing. He said it was better than self-harm, and it kept him safe, and that at least he could feel something – otherwise he was just numb. It gave him some power back when he thought he could choose to do something with his body.

Sometimes people can only feel certain parts of their body, as if other parts have been frozen in time. Rose said, "It's really odd. When I'm at work I can focus on my job unless I'm in meetings when I get incredibly hot and come out in a rash." On some occasions she would nearly pass out or have to leave the meeting and her employer, unsurprisingly, found this irritating. As we worked together, we realised that the meetings took place in small, enclosed rooms, and often with men. This was the situation which triggered the issue. The best defence her body could adopt was to become hot and try to remove her from the situation.

Because the abuser has made the child feel dirty, often feelings are so suppressed that the survivor is unaware of them. It is as if there is no place for feelings, and the survivor asks, "How do I know having feelings is safe?"

Rose said, "The best I can do every day is have a drink to blot it all out; at least then I can have a moment of relief.

I was so busy helping and healing others that I completely forgot about me, and now I am having to deal with the consequences of that, and I am suffering with my body in so many ways. I've no choice now but to have operations, and even though I am still scared, I know that I must do it.

Every night I went out and got drunk, and I was so consumed with trying to deal with my own feelings that I forgot about my child. I'm learning now to take care of her, and as I learn this I'm learning about me and taking care of me and my body."

Rose was using chaos so she would be taken care of.

Laura would often come to the session and start by showing me her latest piercing. This wasn't something she proudly displayed, but rather it was a way of her communicating to me just how bad the week had been for her. It was a barometer of her feelings and a way in which she could hurt herself, just as her abuser had hurt her. She decided that as she must be rubbish to have had that treatment, she might as well carry on being rubbish, and at least she had a tiny amount of control, because she could decide where the piercing would be and what form it could take.

Compulsive eating

Sue said, "I know I'm not hungry, but I'll still get chocolates and crisps on the way home and eat the lot. I don't want to keep doing this, but I've tried lots of diets and just can't stick to them. It's such hard work, but it does give me relief for a few moments."

Overeating (and drinking) can reflect a variety of issues. It can be a way to repress feelings, a way to have a treat and self-nurture, or a way to hide: "When I'm physically big, no one will want me, so I am safe."

On the other hand, if a child was small when abused, when he is in a large body he may feel safe because he is visible and taking up space.

<u>Needing to be heard.</u>

A child who has been abused has kept a secret for a long time, and it's something which is never talked about, even though it affects daily life.

Bodies remember ACTIONS, not just feelings and sensations.

I have a special CD which helps people get their voice back. It consists of warm-up exercises involving singing. Some people may not want to confront the abuser, or it may not be possible. Having the opportunity to be heard, and hearing themselves, is really important. Music can be very helpful – playing a musical instrument, or just making a noise with it. Sometimes this is used to let people start healing by making a noise, and it can be safer if it's done using a musical instrument – it isn't necessary to be able to play music. Dancing can also be used in sessions.

5. BOUNDARIES

<u>What are boundaries?</u>

Boundaries relate to how you are in the world; how you are towards others, and how you are towards yourself. They are concerned with knowing that you are a separate person from another – that you are two distinct people.

We all have to have boundaries. Arriving on time for appointments and paying for goods and services when we said we would are good examples of respecting boundaries. On the other hand, being excessively intrusive would be an example of violating or disrespecting boundaries. You may have had the experience where someone stands too close to you, you move back and they follow you – and when you try to move again, they are still "in your space".

<u>Why are boundaries important?</u>

Boundaries keep us safe and healthy. We may have rigid boundaries for some occasions and flexible boundaries at other times. They help us set personal limits, so we and others are clear what we will and won't do. For example, a friend asks to borrow money, but doesn't ask another friend. Why? It's because he already knows that the other friend will say, "No."

How do I keep myself safe – do I have the right to say "No"?

Eliza was constantly at the beck and call of her family, and even though she became exhausted, she didn't feel able to say "No" to friends and family. She would help to sort out others' problems, listen to friends for hours about their issues, and she was always "on hand". When I asked her, "Eliza, what about you? Do you want to spend most of your life looking after others and not yourself?" she looked stunned, and said it hadn't really occurred to her she had a choice. "It's who I am," she replied.

How do you change to healthy boundaries, and what about fear of rejection?

I asked Eliza what life would be like, and who she would be if she started to notice what she might want, and if she started to build a separate life – a life of her own, in fact. She gulped and looked terrified, and said, "But Josephine, I would have no friends because they would just all abandon me. Saying 'No' is so difficult; it's exhausting, and in the end it's easier to say 'Yes', but then I'm not happy and

I don't get what I want. I ended up making friends who didn't really care about me because I was desperate for someone.

I can be a really good girl and help everyone, but I now realise I've been almost too helpful to try and compensate for the bad person I feel I am. I want to help others where no one helped me, and it's exhausting."

We looked at the easiest situations first and practised saying "No" in therapy. We used many different exercises. A useful exercise to start with is one using string where you lay out the string around you on the floor and you see how far out you would really like the string to stretch in order to know your own personal space. Another exercise helps you know if there is one side of your body more comfortable than another when being close to people. This is something you can try out in a public place – a café, for instance. Move around and see where feels right for you.

How do you know if a relationship or friendship is healthy or unhealthy?

Do you feel empowered or do you feel stuck? Do you feel exhausted in this person's company or uplifted? Are they there for you or is it always you doing the giving?

Barbara had the experience of being "the only person" who could help her new best friend Trudy. Initially she felt special, and in a good close relationship which was something she hadn't had before. She felt she was useful. As time went on, Barbara noticed that she rarely had the chance to talk about herself. She moved on in life, started a part-time job, and began a new relationship with a man. Trudy seemed excited for her and wanted to know all the details. Again Barbara felt special, and said how wonderful it was that someone was there for her. Barbara noticed Trudy was often advising her, especially about her new relationship, and whilst she sometimes felt uneasy about the things she said, she kept thinking that she must have a lot more life experience to be able to advise to such an extent. Barbara felt in a small way as though she finally understood what it would have been like to have had a caring mother.

Early one morning Trudy rang Barbara in an emergency as she often did, but on this particular morning Barbara was on her way to work and said, "Sorry, I'll have to ring you later."

Indeed, Barbara did ring her the minute she arrived home from work, but she was shocked by the conversation. Trudy told her she had done far more for Barbara and that Barbara never appreciated her. She screamed, cried, told a stunned Barbara the exact number of times she had phoned her, and that it was obvious she had never cared anyway.

As Barbara recounted this story, extremely upset and agitated and feeling totally betrayed, we looked at the "red flags" in this relationship. There needs to be a healthy balance of both people's needs. We need to feel we are equal in a relationship.

Barbara said she hadn't really wanted Trudy to keep ringing early in the morning, and that it exhausted her because it was always about Trudy's latest crisis. We looked at why she felt she couldn't say "No", and what *she* might want out of a friendship.

We talked about setting her own rules. Boundaries are needed for friendships going forward, and we established that it's OK to say "No". A healthy friendship is two-way, and we don't need to look after someone else and their feelings. This helps us notice we are all individuals. Barbara hadn't really wanted to discuss all the details of her new relationship, but she felt "obliged" and that she might lose the friendship if she didn't do so. On reflection, she could see that this was a violation of her boundaries, whilst also acknowledging the part she had played in this. In a healthy friendship we can say "No" and expect to be heard and respected for that. We are allowed a separate life because we are individuals. Constantly being woken by early morning phone calls was not only something Barbara didn't want, but it was also exhausting her. She was frightened to say anything, but in a healthy friendship we can be adult and equal with each other.

6. TRIGGER, FLASHBACK

<u>What are they and what causes them?</u>

Triggers and flashbacks often occur together. The trigger reminds us of a past event, and in the flashback we almost relive the event.

A trigger consists of a set of circumstances which sets off a reaction relating to the past, but it feels as though it is happening in the present. Jan went out to a bar one night. The bar was busy, the music was loud, and people were struggling for space. She was jostled accidentally by a man trying to get to the bar. This sent her into fear because it provoked the flashback of a whole series of events from her past. Some years before she had been attacked by a man when she had been walking down a dark street. The trigger for Jan was a man in her personal space touching her.

Triggers were initially part of our defence mechanism and our means of survival. They existed originally as a positive resource. All defences are there for positive reasons in the beginning, but sometimes they become outdated.

There are two types of flashbacks – one where you have intense feelings as if you are actually experiencing the event in the moment, and the other type which occurs consistently over a period of time. Hari said that every time an ambulance went past and she heard the siren, she would stop what she was doing and wonder who had died. This was connected to her mother dying in traumatic circumstances many years earlier. Hari is now 60, and she was 15 when her mother died.

Time does not heal trauma – the old adage that time is a great healer does not apply to trauma. Triggers make us feel that we are in danger NOW rather than we were in danger then.

Do I just avoid the situations that trigger me?

It's not a question of avoiding triggering situations, but rather there is a need to deal with situations one by one at our own pace. We also need to learn how to self soothe.

In therapy we helped Anne to notice and recognise what activates the triggers. After the triggers had been activated she would go to bed, hide and feel numb. We worked on a safety plan, noticing what her window of tolerance was, and we created her own booklet with helpful suggestions for when she couldn't think – suggestions which specifically related to her.

Therapy helps people to learn how to stay in the moment and stay present in the "here and now", and to recognise which situations need to be addressed first to build up confidence in the tools and techniques.

Feelings are not dangerous in themselves; it is only when we perceive they are dangerous that they feel like a threat.

<u>Why is it so hard to help myself?</u>

Triggered feelings are much harder to soothe. In trauma the body reacts first, then processes the issue verbally. Triggered feelings are usually more intense and sudden.

Threat is the *anticipation* of harm, and it does not just occur when violence has taken place.

Jasmine spent a lot of time trying to fight what was going on internally. She often seemed to be looking at "the latest thing", and yet nothing ever seemed to make a difference. Health products (which she took erratically), the latest technique, or a motivational book – nothing seemed to have any impact, but it all gave her an ever increasing overdraft.

The underlying issue was trauma.

7. DISSOCIATION

<u>What is it?</u>

When we cannot physically leave a trauma, or we feel overwhelmed, we may find some way to leave psychologically. Put simply, dissociation is when we are "not all there". In our head we go somewhere else.

Yvonne said to me that as a child, if she wasn't able to leave a place physically, the best she could do was go somewhere else in her head. That is dissociation.

Dissociation is used by trauma survivors to help keep them safe.

James described it as coming out of his body and watching himself from the outside. Others may see split parts of themselves, almost feeling they have different voices in their head (this is different from the internal chatterbox voice, which we all have). Dissociation is used as a way of escaping, both in the moment and as an ongoing strategy to protect ourselves from painful memories.

It is a strange feeling, and one often not talked about, because when we dissociate we feel we are going crazy. Anna said to me that she thought she was developing early dementia, although she was only 26. When I explained what dissociation was and that it was initially to protect herself as a child from abusive events, and that she wasn't in fact "crazy" as she thought, she just cried and said that she thought she was going to end up in a psychiatric ward like her mother. Her relief was palpable.

Dissociation can be described as a fragmented memory; it is as if it's stored in separate boxes. It's the conflict between the parts that causes the problem, rather than the fact that the memory is stored separately.

<u>Why is it a bad thing? How does it affect you?</u>

In dissociation we lose connection with the world. Some people invent a fantasy world, and others have used this to write creatively. Eric said that it was like being outside the body. "I was watching the abuse happening, and it helped me feel no pain, just a numbness. I could go into my own world where no one could do me harm. Sometimes I could see others being hurt, then I could go and rescue them, and for a few moments I would feel better."

<u>What do I do to help with this?</u>

Use the part of you that can get on with life. By this I mean go out, have a routine, go to work if you have a job, go shopping, and partake in everyday life – the ordinary, "boring" stuff of everyday life.

Using mindfulness we can learn how to ground ourselves, looking at an appropriate strategy and establishing what feels achievable now and what are longer-term goals. Sophie and I worked together for some time on this, looking at everything in great detail, and checking what triggers there might be for her. She decided that meeting a friend in a café would be her first goal. She decided on a café, went there on her own, established where in the cafe she felt comfortable, and looked at the menu to decide what she might like to order. Gradually she progressed to feeling comfortable inviting people to a restaurant for a meal. This was something that she had always thought only others could do, and she felt very proud of herself for being able to do this.

8. MEMORY

Usually a memory is recognised as being of an event in the past. A traumatic memory appears to be happening now, in the present.

A lot of what happens in trauma and our subsequent reactions occur below the thinking part of the brain.

Memories are held in the brain, but they are not always accessible to front of mind. Sometimes people say they have no memories and they do not know the reasons behind depression and anxiety symptoms, but the body knows the reasons.

In trauma there may be fragments of memories – the frontal lobe may go off line, but the body still remembers, and it seems hard to make sense of the whole picture.

As our bodies hold memories, we might have a smell that reminds us of a schoolroom, or a perfume that reminds us of a certain night out.

Karen said that she had a bad memory, and as a result was unable to remember details. In therapy there is a need not to overwhelm you, but to allow a small amount of space. When you are ready to process memories it isn't just a question of going over the details; processing helps you move on and put the memory in the past, in a different place in the brain.

Therapy helps you to reach a place where you can observe your memory without reliving it. This is known as dual awareness, and you become mindful of what is happening in your body.

You can hold both past and present in consciousness, so you can say something was awful THEN, not NOW.

Abraham said that one day as he was crossing a busy road, a motorbike came speeding up and almost knocked him down. Now not only is he wary of that road, the sound of motorbikes also makes him jumpy, and he is aware of tensing up his whole body as he is crossing that part of the road.

Marie was a fit and healthy 38-year-old riding instructor. One day her horse bolted and threw her off. She broke her pelvis and was in hospital for a long time. She was then naturally fearful of getting back on a horse. A horse is sensitive to a human body, so Marie had to work hard on her body memory.

Therapy helped Abraham and Marie overcome their issues.

In therapy we help the body to focus on incomplete physical actions – how the body wanted to move in the trauma, but couldn't. Physical movement might be encouraged to focus on what your body wanted to do. Completing the action will help to release the trauma.

9. SHAME

Trauma, especially when experienced in childhood, often results in unjustified feelings of guilt and shame. The survivor can have the false belief that the trauma was his or her fault.

Shame is powerful. We have a strong body response to shame which can immobilise us, and we then criticise ourselves for being "so stupid".

Jean came to see me because she was fed up with the comments from her work colleagues who were always telling her to relax and smile more. "If only I could," she said. The more friends said this, the more self-conscious and shameful she felt. She said all this to me while looking down at the floor, with no eye contact whatsoever. Because shame can immobilise us, we literally sometimes cannot think or speak; it freezes us. Shame may have been a survival strategy used to lessen the intensity of emotions.

As we worked together, I had a sense of a very young child in front of me. As she learned to trust me, she revealed that when growing up she had been constantly criticised by her mother for "not standing straight", and her mother would say to her, "What's wrong with you? Why do I have a child who does not smile like other children? God will give you something to be miserable about." Jean felt angry at herself because she wasn't able to relax, and she despised herself more. Gradually she was able to understand that not only did she feel the shame, but there was also a part of her that was angry at feeling shameful. As we worked together and she learned to become more compassionate for the shameful part of her, seeing it as just a part of her whole character, she started to be able to look people in the eye, and she found she could smile more. She started to understand what "feeling relaxed" actually meant.

Tilly came to me because she had tried various self-help programmes to help promote positive thinking. She couldn't understand why these programmes seemed to be making her feel worse. She said, "I listen to these recordings and then mentally beat myself up for being so stupid – I can't take it in." Tilly had a real light bulb moment when we looked at which part of her was trying to protect her from hearing praise; she realised it was the part of her that had been shamed. In trauma we split off or put away certain parts of our self. To keep Tilly feeling safe, the shame part was cut off.

"But there must be something about me or something that I was doing because I was abused by several people," she said. After one incidence of abuse, boundaries are blurred and you become more vulnerable.

Tilly was not aware of what boundaries really meant.

Shame always has a physical impact on the body; it does not just affect the mind. It's a lonely, terrifying place. Early shame means we are vulnerable as we grow up; we may withdraw, or even use anger to keep others at a safe distance. Shame paralyses both body and mind.

Hannah said, "Can people see that I've been abused? I feel so ugly and dirty as if everyone knows. I have a terrible memory, so perhaps there are things I've done I don't know about. I'm so clumsy all the time, I'm just useless. Just going out shopping is a big ordeal for me. I can't have friends because I will never be able to go out with them, and the few people I've met have soon got fed up of me. They make excuses or just let me down. It's so hard and lonely. A friend asked me why I never wear makeup, and she said I'd be so pretty if I did. That sent me reeling into chaos for weeks. Abuse isn't something you can tell anyone. It's dirty, I'm dirty."

10. ANGER

Anger is a natural feeling, but it is important to cope with it effectively. In trauma, survivors can feel ashamed of their anger, and in other cases anger provides a false sense of strength.

Anger can show itself at any time after a traumatic event. Years after the event it can remain buried in the body if not dealt with. Issues associated with anger include ignoring it, taking the anger out on others, or simply taking it out on yourself in a destructive way.

We have a way of hiding anger, but in turn this can lead to our hating ourselves, and then destructive thought and behaviour blaming ourselves can be prominent.

Sam, 27, came to see me with anger issues. At the age of seven he had experienced a trauma when his father left him. The aggressive nature of his parents' splitting up made this particularly traumatic. He didn't see his father again for many years.

During his therapy sessions the anger surprisingly came last, because what came first was the rejection. "Why did he leave me? Did he love me? How could my father do this to me? I am alone."

Behind the anger there were the other feelings of loneliness and rejection which came to the surface, and they had to be dealt with first.

In cases of abuse anger is often not able to be attributed to the abuser for all sorts of reasons, and the anger becomes turned inwards or starts to overwhelm.

Sam was living abroad when the trauma occurred, and he only felt safe enough to explore the anger when he was back living in this country. He knew he simply had to contain his feelings and get himself home safely, so he started drinking heavily to suppress his feelings.

"But I don't want to stop getting angry," Margaret said, even though she was in danger of losing her job. "It keeps me safe, and it's the only way I know how to be in the world, although it is exhausting."

Sometimes we replace one feeling with another; Margaret had replaced vulnerability with anger. It may be that in a family no one expressed sadness, but there was always a lot of anger, so the family members learned that expressing anger was OK, even though they really wanted to express sadness. "I feel like there's two of me in my body. One part of me feels very destructive and angry." It's not about getting rid of that part – it is about the protection it is affording in a healthy way.

Anger often comes to the fore when we feel safe enough in the therapeutic relationship to start to express our true feelings, and for most this can be a while after therapy was first undertaken.

"I have buried anger, but do I have the right to express it? Once I start to express it, I won't be able to stop."

We might think that if anger goes, power will go too. Anger in itself is not bad; it's how you cope with the anger that affects your life.

Often someone who has experienced trauma feels angry. Have you done anything harmful to yourself or others as a result of anger?

It may be that there are angry parts of us that have not yet learned how to think and deal with anger in healthy ways.

Having the right to say "No" is important. You need to experiment with the language that is right for you, and you will then know which words to use when.

"It took me a long time to know I had the right to get angry, to know I was a worthwhile enough person to get angry. Does it mean I have to forgive too?"

Is anger ever appropriate?

Anger can be healthy; it's not just destructive. "My parents were always angry. Does that mean I'm as bad as they were if I allow myself to become angry?" You can become angry at the child part of you – the child who had no choice but to "put up and shut up". Anger can be healthy, but violence is never healthy. Anger and violence are different.

It's perfectly understandable that there is a fear of expressing anger. You need to learn how to do this safely, and how to be assertive – to know you have a voice which can be heard.

John, aged 75, had had many broken relationships. He cared enough about his current girlfriend to decide finally that he needed to find out what he could do to replace violence. He said, "I'm sick of the old round of violence, stormy relationships, and moving on to the next one."

He told me that he was unable to control his anger. We looked at his anger style which was always to escalate the anger rather than manage it. Some of it was learned behaviour from his father, who, although never physically abusive, would throw objects and break things.

"I have meltdowns. My heart beats wildly, my breathing is rapid, and I can't think straight. I become a horrible person; it's like there's a monster inside me. I wish it would stop. It feels as though it comes out of the blue and hijacks my life. I just feel so exhausted afterwards, and start beating myself up for being such a horrible person."

There are many ways in which I would recommend addressing this. Write a letter – which you do NOT send – with your non-dominant hand, using as many swear words as you want. It can then be brought to the session for therapist to see before being burned or torn up.

Art therapy can be used. I have specially designed pictures for this.

Go to the top of a hill and shout. If you shout as if you are looking for a dog, no one thinks this is strange.

The two-chair technique can be employed, but I only recommend this is done under the guidance of a therapist, as this is VERY powerful.

Therapeutic voice techniques can also be employed.

11. SELF-ESTEEM

Self-esteem is the degree to which you value yourself. It can also be described as faith in yourself, pride, and self-assurance.

Our sense of identity comes from our parents. When you are abused you lose your sense of identity.

Cynthia was 33 when she first came to see me. She started by saying, "I don't know what's wrong with me, but I know there is another person in here struggling to get out. I know that sounds crazy, but please can you help me?" Cynthia had started her own business and kept sabotaging herself by not keeping appointments. She said that she wanted to work but was afraid of "being seen".

"If I start to look nice and feminine, I just feel disgusted with myself. I would put nice makeup on and then scrub it all off. My friends think I have an allergy and keep trying to find different types of makeup for me to wear. I can't tell them I feel like a slut when I wear makeup."

Cynthia had a fear of moving forward.

"I kept making decisions in life that were so wrong for me, yet at the same time I was terrified of making the wrong decision. I just felt stuck and trapped all the time. I wanted to stay indoors, draw the curtains and hide away. How could I go out? People would see me. Suppose I had a panic attack? The shame of it.

It took me a very long time before I knew I could ask for help. Partly my self-esteem was so low – who would help me? – and partly I didn't trust anyone. Little by little I tried small things, and sometimes I would get knocked back."

If a trauma is not dealt with, it can cause other problems, and our self-perception becomes tarnished.

Susan was 47 and had suffered mental, sexual and physical abuse from her parents for ten years from the age of nine.

"I remember I looked in the mirror two years after the abuse and I could not recognise who I was. All I saw was that I was ugly and I had changed in my appearance, yet I was only 21. I said, 'Who am I? I feel unloved and unlovable.' I felt ugly and a great need to hide away."

What became apparent was that part of her didn't feel like an adult, and she didn't know how to behave in an adult world. Although 47, inside she still felt nine years old.

What was also apparent was that in her daily life she struggled with simple daily activities, confrontations and adult decisions. Decisions became too difficult and a great sense of hiding away and strong feelings of fear as an adult became prominent. These took over her life before she received therapy.

She could not feel or did not want to interact with any form of happiness. She felt numb, and avoided parties and family gatherings where she would have to put on a show.

Theresa said, "I feel like I don't belong. I feel like an alien. I feel as though I have to put a mask on to try and survive."

Pam said, "How can I honestly say I was abused, when I kept going back every week? Part of me fancied him, and he gave me lots of attention and treats."

When I asked Pam how old she was at the time, she told me she was 11 and he was 16. Abuse can take place because the abuser develops a relationship with you, makes you feel special, and gives you treats. It doesn't matter whether it was because it was something you weren't getting at home, or whether your parents were simply too busy; it is still abuse, and you were not responsible. People become really confused about the fact that they got treats and enjoyed them. This is exactly what the abuser intended.

"I'd love to meet someone and be happy, but I just keep meeting the wrong sort of person. The people I meet are abusive and controlling. Do I not deserve love?"

When I met Cath at a women's refuge, she was really frustrated and fed up with herself. She complained bitterly that "there are no nice guys", or at least she never found them. She felt as though she had no entitlement to be happy. That's for other people, she thought, and "Anyway, I'd probably be bored," she added as she was heading to the door at the end of the first session.

"I hear other people say love yourself first. I just don't know what that means. Please can you explain that to me?

I think I'm probably just a really bad person and it feels like there is something in me that needs to be removed or dug out. But I kept putting up with the abuse, so does that not make me an abuser too? I was 14 and could have said 'No'".

There are NO circumstances in which a child is responsible for abuse. NONE.

Abusers are very good at making the abuse a "special secret"; perhaps that's the only time they themselves get to feel special. Our bodies are like machines to a certain extent and will react to certain physical touch.

"I have lots of really weird bizarre dreams that often worry me; what about that? I'm so angry in my dreams that I'm really scared I must be a bad person and that I really will end up harming someone."

Fran was 48 and a highly successful businesswoman who came to see me initially because of sleep issues; she worked very long hours, and achieving and being the best she could be was central to her life.

Initially we talked about her daily life, and the earlier years, and what she thought might be causing her to be so driven.

It is much too terrifying to talk about abuse without having built up some trust. As we talked about her history, it soon became apparent that the nightmares had been occurring for many years, and always with the theme of a dark figure. Fran said she had "perfect parents". Of course there are good parents, but no one is perfect and that lack of realism is a clue in itself. Often we adopt this stance in order to protect ourselves because it's very hard to admit that the very people who are supposed to love and look after you have abused and harmed you.

Silence about trauma leads to the death of the soul.

12. SPIRITUALITY

Spirituality is a deep feeling of being connected with our innate spirit and energy. It helps us thrive rather than escape from reality.

I think the best way to describe spirituality is that this is the love I have for myself or the love of self and others. Spirituality is what we perceive love with God to be or, if we don't believe in God, the love we feel is available to us from whatever source we find relevant.

Our choices and life experiences affect our perception, especially on spiritual matters.

Self could be described as the heart centre; memories are gathered from childhood and they affect how we perceive matters of the heart.

Trauma can cause the heart link to our spirituality to become numb or frozen meaning that normal feelings of love may not be felt.

The heart connects to every part of us – mental, physical and emotional. Sometimes after experiencing trauma these functions are separated.

- Physical Pain

- Emotional Pain

- Low Self-esteem

- Depression

The heart connects these functions, and one or all of the functions become extremely active at different times, during and after trauma therapy.

Trauma affects the muscles of the body – including the heart. Its function is to love. Trauma can cause the heart to be locked.

"Cold as ice", "Heart as hard as a stone", "Heart wrapped in chains" – these are all expressions which have been said by people who have experienced a broken heart through trauma.

I hope this brief booklet has been helpful and you realise that trauma can be overcome and there is help available.

Please do not hesitate to contact me if I can help you on your healing journey.

www.jmcpsychotherapy.com

Printed in Great Britain
by Amazon.co.uk, Ltd.,
Marston Gate.